CW01559111

Battle of the
World War II

A History from Beginning to End

Copyright © 2019 by Hourly History.

Table of Contents

Introduction

The annals of World War II resound with names like Pearl Harbor, Dunkirk, Bastogne, Midway, Stalingrad, Berlin, Iwo Jima, and many others in a geography that defined the story of the battle between the Allied and the Axis Powers. And yet, British Prime Minister Winston Churchill knew better than anyone that the Battle of the Atlantic was to be the dominating factor from the beginning of the war in September 1939 until Germany was defeated in May 1945.

It was Churchill who christened history's longest and most complicated naval battle the Battle of the Atlantic. While Europe nervously waited through the Phoney War, the Battle of the Atlantic was where the naval contest actually got underway. Allies and Axis alike saw their lives end in watery graves, as more than 75,000 Allied seamen and 18,000 U-boat crew members died during the campaign, which began on the first day of World War II and ended on the last day of the global conflict that forever altered history.

More than 2,000 merchant ships sank, and 70% of Germany's submarines met their demise in the Atlantic. Thousands of ships engaged in over 100 convoy battles and as many as 1,000 encounters between single ships across 3,000 square miles of the Atlantic Ocean. As Churchill noted, had the Atlantic not emerged as a success for the Allies, the invasion of Normandy and the landings in Europe would have been doomed.

After declaring war against Nazi Germany on September 3, 1939, the Allies began the blockade of

Germany. In retaliation, the Nazis launched a counter-blockade. Throughout the war, victory would shift from one side to the other as the Atlantic witnessed its most volatile martial engagement ever.

The Germans were intent on blockading Europe to the point of complete capitulation, and they were counting on their U-boats to make it happen. In addition to the U-boats, the Germans had other warships of the Kriegsmarine or Navy, as well as the powerful Luftwaffe providing support from the air. They also had submarines of the Italian Royal Navy after Italy entered the war on the side of Germany on June 10, 1940. The Allies would eventually include the British, Canadian, and American navies, along with merchant shipping. The Allied merchant ships that were crossing the Atlantic did so in convoys, escorted by destroyers and corvettes. It fell to the British and Canadian ships and airplanes to guard the convoys which were heading to Great Britain and the Soviet Union from North America. American ships and planes joined in the convoys on September 13, 1941, almost three months before the Japanese attacked Pearl Harbor.

Great Britain's dependence on imported goods made the nation vulnerable. To be able to fight, the British needed over a million tons of imported material a week; it was up to the Allies to keep Britain supplied, while it was the goal of Germany and its Axis partners to bring a halt to the shipping on its way to Great Britain. Knowing that the eventual intention of the Allied control of the Atlantic was the invasion of mainland Europe, Germany was determined to prevent the Allies from building up supplies and equipment in Great Britain.

The U-boats sank almost a half a million tons of the precious Allied shipping that ended up at the bottom of the North Atlantic. German battlecruisers *Scharnhorst* and *Gneisenau* managed to either destroy or capture 22 ships for a total of 115,600 tons of shipping in two months alone. The *Bismarck*, newly built and reputed to be the most powerful of the German warships, was poised to turn its attention to the transatlantic convoys that had already endured U-boats as well as land-based bombers.

While the French remained in the war, they were able to join with their British allies to maintain a long-range blockade that was fairly effective. This initial phase of the Battle for the Atlantic, which began in the fall of 1939, was dealt a severe blow when, against all expectations of the Allies, France fell to the German invaders. Great Britain, which had lost its ally, also suffered from losses that the Germans had inflicted upon its naval forces as the British retreated from Norway and evacuated from Dunkirk. Because the Nazis were able to prevent the British from using the direct route from the Mediterranean Sea to the Suez Canal, British ships were obliged to travel around the Cape of Good Hope, a much longer route. The cargo-carrying capacity of the British merchant marine was cut nearly in half at a time when Germany had acquired naval and air bases on the coast of the Atlantic, putting the Nazis in place to deliver even more devastating attacks upon the shipping.

Germany, buoyed by its easy conquest of Western Europe, was confident that it would be no great difficulty to attack British trade on the waters and force Great Britain out of the war. Their early success with U-boat attacks bore out this optimism. But somehow, the joined forces of Germany's U-boats, air, and surface forces were not able to drive the British to surrender. Luck seemed to hold with the British as the Canadian naval and air forces were able to support a transatlantic convoy system by May 1941.

The United States, still not an active partner in the war, was able to provide a form of support through its Lend-Lease program which took effect in 1940. In exchange for 50 American World War I destroyers, Great Britain gave the United States 99-year leases for bases in Bermuda and various places in the Caribbean as well as Newfoundland.

The United States joined the war in December 1941; with Americans engaged in the Pacific theater of the war, the Germans capitalized upon the unguarded shipping off the East Coast of the U.S. Between January and June 1942, Allied merchant shipping losses soared, and more tonnage was lost during that time than the Allies had lost in the previous two and a half years. Along the South Atlantic, the U-boats were effective along the shipping lanes to Asia and the Middle East, forcing the Allies to rely upon seaborne supplies that were shipped in the dangerous waters where the U-boats prowled from 1942-1943. The Nazis were also effective in endangering Allied convoys headed for Russian ports, attacking from the air and under the water.

But Canada came to the rescue in the North Atlantic as American forces headed to the Caribbean and the Pacific. It was the Canadians who established the first convoys in the American zone., and it was the Royal Canadian Navy that escorted the transatlantic convoys as they shifted their western terminus from Halifax to New York City in September 1942. The year 1942 saw the convoy system acquiring more strength and improved equipment and, by autumn of 1942, the Americans ramped up their merchant shipbuilding and began gaining on the losses that had been suffered earlier in the battle.

By late 1942, with the U-boats forced back to the mid-Atlantic by the convoy system in the Western Hemisphere, the battle surged. In March, the British intelligence program, named Ultra, failed in intercepting and decrypting U-boat communication in mid-ocean, providing the Germans with success as they sighted every Allied convoy and attacked half of them. However, the tide of battle was shifting by 1943 and reinforcements were pouring into the North Atlantic to provide naval and air support. As the weather improved in April, the advantages of the modern Allied radar, penetration of U-boat codes, new escort aircraft carriers, and very-long-range patrol aircraft, as well as more aggressive methods saw Germany's submarine fleet suffer a stunning defeat by May 1943.

Unable to achieve success through acoustic-homing torpedoes, the U-boats utilized a guerilla campaign by retreating inshore to try to stop the shipping. But the Allies were winning the Atlantic and, as the Mediterranean opened later in 1943, the Allies suffered fewer shipping losses. The rest of the war saw the Allies able to maintain their control of the sea lanes of the Atlantic. The Atlantic Ocean, from the opening of the Battle of the Atlantic to the Allied invasion of Normandy, was a dangerous front line of battle for the navies of both sides of the conflict.

Chapter One

The Threat of the German U-Boats

"The only thing that ever really frightened me during the war was the U-boat peril."

—Winston Churchill

Despite the effectiveness of the U-boats in World War I, neither the British nor the Germans had carried that memory into their preparations for World War II. When the Battle of the Atlantic began, the Germans were using mostly surface vessels to patrol the Atlantic Ocean. However, on September 3, 1939, when war was declared, a German U-boat torpedoed the British liner *Athenia*. It was an apt beginning for the Battle of the Atlantic, a campaign which was the longest battle of the war and which, in effect, picked up nautically where World War I had left off.

The British depended upon the merchant ships that transported oil, food, raw materials, equipment, and troops from North America to Great Britain. If the U-boats managed to bring a halt to the convoys, Great Britain would be depleted of its supplies and could be forced out of the war.

The U-boat commander, Admiral Karl Dönitz, had gained his submarine experience from the previous world war and his forces were well trained. He, unlike the other German admirals, was convinced that the U-boats would prove to be an extremely effective force against the British sea lines of communication (SLOC). However, Dönitz was a tactician who was not interested in the ways that technology could enhance the impact of his offensive. The measurement that he was interested in was the amount of merchant ship tonnage that could be sunk by the U-boats. He also expected British convoys to be easy to locate because he felt that most of the fighting would take place near Great Britain. With a central, land-based command headquarters to control the U-boats, the Battle of the Atlantic would, Dönitz was sure, be a German victory.

Had the Germans opted to prepare for the war by taking part in war games, Dönitz might have recognized the operational difficulties that lay in store for the U-boats in the campaign. Because the British increased the number of their anti-submarine forces, the coastal area around Great Britain would prove to be too dangerous for the U-boats, forcing the SLOCs to move out into the open Atlantic. There, the convoys would have more maneuvering room, and the U-boats would find it a challenge to concentrate their attacks as a group, which was part of the plan that Dönitz favored. By the end of 1940, the wolf pack tactic that Admiral Karl Dönitz introduced managed to diminish the effectiveness of ASDIC (an early version of sonar) when U-boats surfaced as a group during the night to launch their attack.

The small, Type VII U-boats that Dönitz favored, designed to be used off the British coast, lacked the range that would be needed later in the war to reach America's

East Coast. The Type IX U-boat was larger and did have the range to stay on the East Coast for longer periods of time; nonetheless, the Germans throughout the war built three times as many of the smaller craft. In the first year of the war, only 35 new boats were available for service, and 28 of those were lost at sea.

Still, just as the flying aces of World War I had risen to fame above the skies, the Germans had U-boat aces under the water for World War II. Günther Prien of *U-47*, Otto Kretschmer of *U-99*, Engelbert Endrass of *U-46*, Victor Oehrn of *U-37*, Heinrich Bleichrodt of *U-48*, and Joachim Schepke of *U-100* were the aces of the undersea as their U-boats attacked the British convoys. The German U-boat *Rudel* or wolf pack attacks began in September and October of 1940; the British lost 11 of its 42 merchant vessels during that brief time period. The wolf packs were coordinated by radio, since the Germans had broken the British Naval Cypher No. 3 and knew at what time and in what place the convoys would be located. Spreading out in a patrol line that could cut the Allied convoy route in half, the crews would then use binoculars to look for masts or smoke against the horizon; failing that, they could pick up propeller sounds through hydrophones.

Luftwaffe planes sank more than 300,000 tons of British shipping during 1940-1941. To the Germans, this period was known as "the first happy time" as the success of the U-boats foretold a successful destiny for their war efforts. They knew that if they were able to prevent the Allies from moving vessels in the North Atlantic, there would be no hope of advancing Allied ground efforts against the Germans in the Mediterranean, or mounting a successful invasion upon German-occupied Europe.

The invasion and occupation of France in 1940 was a boon to the Germans in their quest to own the Atlantic, providing them with access to the major French naval ports at Brest, Bordeaux, Saint-Nazaire, and Cherbourg. Their triumph in Norway also yielded the benefits of Norwegian ports. Because these ports were closer to the mid-Atlantic than many of the British ports, the Germans were able to redefine the boundaries of the Battle for the Atlantic. Acquiring these forward bases increased U-boat range and allowed the long-range aircraft like the Focke-Wulf Fw 200 "Kondor" to patrol the Atlantic, attacking shipping as it crossed the ocean, and to do reconnaissance for the U-boats.

The British had been confident that their sonar, ASDIC, would give them the upper hand in the naval campaign. They did have some success when they sank the German *Graf Spee* in December 1939, and also against the *Bismarck* in 1941, but despite this the U-boat crews' "happy time" saw 270 Allied ships sink to the ocean from June to October 1940.

The British need for escort ships for its vital shipping was desperate, but it would not be eased until the United States, which was still neutral, and Great Britain agreed on the Lend-Lease terms which provided the Royal Navy with World War I destroyers in exchange for leases on bases located in British territory. The British were already multitasking at a furious rate. Because of the threat of a German invasion throughout the summer and autumn of 1940, the British fleet had to position 35 destroyers at

Harwich and 35 near Plymouth and Portsmouth so that both ends of the English Channel had protection. The result was fewer anti-submarine escorts for its SLOCs, and a subsequent loss of ships and merchant sailors. Great Britain was in great danger of succumbing to the Germans just as France had done.

Chapter Two

Battleships and the *Bismarck*

*"We'll find that German battleship that's makin' such a
fuss
We gotta sink the Bismarck 'cause the world depends on
us
Hit the decks a-runnin' boys and spin those guns around
When we find the Bismarck we gotta cut her down."*

—Johnny Horton, "Sink the Bismarck"

When England and France declared war on Germany in
1939, the commander-in-chief of the German Navy or
Kriegsmarine, Admiral Erich Raeder, confided in his war
diary that his navy was not prepared to take on the British
in a naval battle. It was, he wrote, too weak, with only 26
submarines available to be used in the Atlantic. "They can
only show that they know how to die with honor," he stated
glumly. While Raeder acknowledged that since 1935, the
Germans had created a well-trained force that could be
used in the Atlantic, the fleet was too few in number
compared to the British.

Such gloomy predictions would not have been shared
by the confident chancellor of Germany, Adolf Hitler.
Hitler had begun planning for a military build-up only four

days after he became Germany's chancellor in January 1933. No expense was to be spared as Germany's rearmament program, crippled by the prohibitions of the Versailles Treaty, got underway. Seeking a fleet of battleships and heavy cruisers, Raeder did not give much credence to the thought that aircraft carriers, which he dismissed as mere "gasoline tankers," would be able to play a dominant role in the war.

Hitler had approved the Kriegsmarine's building plans to create a fleet of battleships, cruisers, and aircraft carriers that would rival that of Great Britain. Admiral Karl Dönitz, commander of the German U-boats, believed that his forces could easily decimate the British surface fleet at a faster rate than they could be replaced. Submarines were easier to build and operate than a large surface fleet. They could operate under the water without being detected and then strike without warning. But the Kriegsmarine disagreed with his views. Germany advanced its military buildup but not to the point of greatly expanding its U-boat fleet.

To an extent, the British had been lulled into a curious lethargy by the Phoney War which followed the German invasion of Poland in September 1939. They were not heeding the warnings of a young military analyst named Harry Hinsley whose analysis of the Kriegsmarine's warships alerted him that the Germans were not idle during this time. Hinsley predicted that a major operation was about to be launched in Scandinavia, but the British paid no heed. That made it possible for the Germans to move into the major ports of Norway without detection by the Royal Navy. The Germans were on the move.

In June 1940, Hinsley noticed that the *Gneisenau* and *Scharnhorst*, two German battlecruisers, were operating off the North Cape of Norway. Again, his warnings were ignored, and as a result, the British carrier *Glorious*, its pilots, Hurricanes, and two destroyers were sunk by the Germans. The British managed to retaliate by torpedoing the battlecruisers and knocking them out of action until December. Hitler had told Admiral Raeder that he would need the cruisers for his planned invasion of Great Britain at the end of the summer, but by that time, only a few destroyers and one heavy cruiser were operational for the Germans.

By January 1941, the *Gneisenau* and the *Scharnhorst* were back in active service and able to raid the sea lines of communications or SLOCs along the North Atlantic coast of Great Britain. Their success forced the British to guard their precious convoys with battleships. The Germans were able to sink 115,000 tons of shipping. Then, in March 1941, the British torpedoed the *Gneisenau*.

But the Germans had a new battleship, the *Bismarck*, which Admiral Raeder sent into action in the Atlantic in May 1941. Accompanying the *Bismarck* was the heavy cruiser *PrinzEugen*. In the early morning on May 19, the *Bismarck* set out on its maiden voyage. It was the first full-scale battleship built by the German Navy since World War I, and the *Prinz Eugen* was the largest warship afloat. They were on a secret mission, Operation Rheinübung, and their purpose was to attack the convoys carrying oil, food, and supplies across the ocean from the U.S. to Great Britain. This was to be the death blow, the Nazis believed, which would cut the supply line for the Allies and force the British to give up or starve.

Informed that the *Bismarck* was in the Atlantic, the British sent a fleet to track it down, including the celebrated HMS *Hood* and the newly commissioned battleship HMS *Prince of Wales*. The *Hood*, which had been launched in 1918, was the largest battle cruiser in the British fleet and its reputation had brought it fame. The British were confident that it would be able to bring down the great *Bismarck*.

On May 24, 1941, the two ships entered the Denmark Strait between Greenland and Iceland. After locating the German ships, the *Hood* fired first with shells traveling 2,000 miles an hour. The commander of the German fleet, Admiral Günther Lütjens, proved indecisive at the attack but, seeing the *Hood* close in, the *Bismarck*'s Captain Ernst Lindemann ordered the *Bismarck* to return fire. For four minutes, the two titans of the ocean exchanged fire, until the *Bismarck*'s shells, ripping through the *Hood*'s deck, hit close to the main tower. An armor-piercing shell tore into the *Hood*'s ammunition magazine, setting off an explosion that sent a pillar of fire 600 feet into the air. The *Hood* broke in two and sank as the crew of the *Prince of Wales* watched in horror. Only 3 members of the 1,421 crew of the *Hood* could be rescued from the water, making the sinking of the *Hood* the largest loss of British life ever suffered from a single naval vessel.

Despite his advantage, Lütjens could not pursue the *Prince of Wales* because the *Bismarck*, with its ruptured tank, was taking on seawater and leaking oil. He intended to bring the *Bismarck* to safety to a port in France, now under Nazi occupation. But the British wanted revenge for the loss of the *Hood*, and Admiral John Tovey called on all of the ships in the British Home Fleet to find and intercept the *Bismarck* before it could find safety.

By May 26, 1941, the *Bismarck* was 12 hours away from a point where it could have Luftwaffe air cover. Tovey ordered an attack from the aircraft carrier HMS *ArkRoyal*. British bombers took off from the deck, zeroed in on their target, and launched torpedoes—but on the HMS *Sheffield*, one of their own ships that was following the *Bismarck*. Luckily, the failure of the torpedoes to detonate prevented a lethal and tragic accident.

After having re-armed on the *Ark Royal*, the pilots flew low to prevent the *Bismarck's* crew from being able to train their guns. The British torpedoes struck the *Bismarck* in its undefended rudders, tearing a huge hole in its hull and disabling its steering mechanisms. Crippled by the attack, the *Bismarck* was now only able to sail in large circles. The night passed with the doomed ship surrounded by the British, who waited until morning to continue the attack to prevent another friendly fire accident.

As dawn broke on May 27, three British warships opened fire on the helpless *Bismarck*. The British ships diminished the distance between them and the *Bismarck* until they were only 3,000 yards away. The HMS *Dorsetshire* fired the final torpedoes upon the *Bismarck* at around 10:20 am. The *Bismarck* sank 20 minutes later, either because of British torpedoes or the German decision to scuttle its "unsinkable" ship. The mighty *Bismarck*, ten days after its maiden voyage, descended to the bottom of the Atlantic Ocean. The British rescued 110 German sailors from the water but had to leave 2,000 men behind as they received word that a U-boat had been sighted.

The loss of the battleship was a grave disappointment to Hitler. He was not encouraged by the performances of the pocket battleship *Lützow* or the heavy cruiser *Admiral Hipper,* which could only bring down one destroyer in a convoy that was protected by six destroyers and two corvettes. Hitler broke up the surface fleet and replaced Raeder with Admiral Karl Dönitz, who persuaded Hitler to rescind the order to decommission the Navy. The order made little difference, however, as the surface ships contributed little to Germany's efforts to subdue the Allies in the Atlantic.

Late in December 1943, the *Scharnhorst* was sunk by the British battleship *Duke of York* off North Cape. The *Tirpitz* was sunk in November 1944 in a Norwegian fjord by three 12,000-pound Tallboy bombs dropped by Bomber Command Lancasters. Except for its U-boats, the Kriegsmarine was not faring well in the Battle of the Atlantic. But if the U-boats could maintain their edge, that could be enough to devastate the Allied convoys.

Chapter Three

The Lend-Lease Program

*"In the present world situation of course there is absolutely
no doubt in the mind of a very overwhelming number of
Americans that the best immediate defense of the United
States is the success of Great Britain in defending itself;
and that, therefore, quite aside from our historic and
current interest in the survival of democracy, in the world
as a whole, it is equally important from a selfish point of
view of American defense, that we should do everything to
help the British Empire to defend itself."*

—Franklin Delano Roosevelt

For the embattled British, 1940 was the grim start to a
tumultuous decade. The Phoney War that began in 1939
with the German invasion of Poland drew Great Britain, as
well as France, into the war against Germany, but when the
Germans invaded France and the French surrendered, Great
Britain stood alone against a predatory and greedy foe
intent on bringing the British to their knees. The French
had had the fourth largest Navy in the world, and although
the Free French Forces joined the fight against the
Germans, they had comparatively few ships with which to
fight. The loss of French ships meant that Great Britain's
fleet had no choice but to extend itself vast miles across the
enormous Atlantic Ocean. Then, with Italy joining the war

against the Allies, the British had to reinforce the Mediterranean Fleet and, in the Western Mediterranean, establish Force H at Gibraltar to replace the French.

The German U-boats did not concentrate their efforts on the shallow English Channel which, by the middle of 1940, was partially blocked by minefields. Instead, the U-boats sailed around the British Isles; German bases at Brest, Lorient, and La Pallice were 450 miles closer to the Atlantic than the bases on the North Sea, enabling the submarines to double their effective size, spend longer on patrol, and attack convoys farther west. Beginning in July 1940, the U-boats, after completing their patrols in the Atlantic, returned to their new French bases. The concrete submarine pens that the Germans built for their U-boats in the French Atlantic were immune to Allied bombing for most of the war and were not vulnerable until the middle of 1944 when the Tallboy bomb changed the dynamics.

The beleaguered Royal Navy of Great Britain, suffering from the loss of seven destroyers after the failed Norway campaign and six destroyers following the evacuation of Dunkirk, and then ten more in the English Channel and the North Sea, was aware that, following the successful conquest of Western Europe by the Nazis, Germany had its sights set on an invasion of Great Britain. For Hitler, the easy victory over the Low Countries and France meant that his U-boats were free to return to the Atlantic and resume their attack on the convoys.

The British had entered the war at a naval disadvantage. The Navy had insufficient long-range escorts capable of protecting ocean-going shipping. The Great Depression that had gripped the world economy during the 1930s had led to cuts in the military budget. Naval spending, instead of going to anti-submarine ships and weapons, went into the battle fleet because the British assumed that the German U-boats would be designed for coastal craft that would threaten the approaches of the harbor. The Royal Air Force Coastal Command's patrol aircraft didn't have the range to cover the North Atlantic; if they saw a U-boat dive, all they could do was use their machine-guns on that location.

Prime Minister Winston Churchill, who had assumed leadership of the British government in May 1940, contacted President Franklin D. Roosevelt of the United States. Roosevelt knew that his nation was not yet ready to engage in the conflict, but he also was aware that neutrality would only be able to last for a limited amount of time. So when he received the request from Churchill for the United States to lend 50 World War I destroyers in exchange for 99-year leases on British bases in Bermuda, the Caribbean, and Newfoundland, President Roosevelt was able to present the deal as a win for the Americans.

The Lend-Lease Act passed on March 11, 1941. It enabled the U.S. to provide military aid to foreign nations and authorized Roosevelt to transfer arms and defense materials to nations whose defense was viewed as vital to American national security. Strategically, the transfer of these supplies without financial compensation from the Soviet Union, Great Britain, Brazil, China, and other nations let the Americans provide war support and protect its own interests without actually engaging in battle. As there were no payments involved, the transfer of war materiel did not violate the 1939 Neutrality Act. Roosevelt deftly dodged any neutrality violations by declaring these weapons and ammunition as surplus so that they could be shipped to the British without financial complications and without ruffling the isolationist leanings of the Americans.

Still, American isolationists were wary. The bill, they asserted, gave the president the power to support war efforts across the globe without actually issuing a declaration of war. As long as there were not American soldiers fighting, neutrality was not violated. They recognized that this seemingly straightforward process was bringing the U.S. gradually into the war. Also, because the dominant ethnic group in the American population was German-Americans, Roosevelt needed to tread carefully

Officially titled "An Act Further to Promote the Defense of the United States," the program was administered under the new Office of Lend-Lease Administration. Franklin D. Roosevelt, the genial, wily strategist who was elected to serve as president for four terms, explained the Lend-Lease program in terms which cleverly avoided a militaristic metaphor. What if his neighbor's house caught fire and the neighbor asked to borrow his garden hose to put it out? "I don't want $15—I want my garden hose back after the fire is over. . . . If it goes through the fire all right, intact, without any damage to it, he gives it back to me and thanks me very much for the use of it." Instead of asking the neighbor to pay for the hose, Roosevelt explained, he just wanted the hose back after the fire was put out.

It would, however, be many months before the old destroyers would be of use in the Battle of the Atlantic. First, they needed to be upgraded to fight a modern war. British and Canadian crews assumed control of the first of the destroyers in September 1940 and proceeded to re-arm them and fit them with ASDIC.

ASDIC, or sonar, played a vital role in the Battle of the Atlantic. ASDIC was able to produce a range and bearing that were accurate with regard to the target, but its ability to interpret could be duped by something as ordinary as the current or even schools of fish. Effective only at low speeds, the system's capabilities were diminished when the ship's speed went above 15 knots because the noise of the ship as it traveled through the water drowned out the echoes. Early ASDIC sets couldn't view from a directly downward perspective, leading the operator to lose contact with the U-boat just as the attack was in the final stages.

In the beginning, the procedure was to sweep the ASDIC from one side of the escort's course to the other in an arc, stopping after a few degrees to emit a signal. If an echo were detected and it was identified by the operator as a submarine, the escort would aim toward the target, plotting the U-boat's range and bearing to determine the course and speed. When nearing the 1,000-yard mark, the decision needed to be made whether or not to attack. If the attack was okayed, the escort would adjust its own course by using the course of speed data of the target. In order to disable the U-boat, the escort had to explode a depth charge within 20 feet. Despite these difficulties in protecting themselves, Allied convoys had no choice but to transport goods across the ocean. U-boats remained the fierce predator of the Battle of the Atlantic.

The assistance provided by the United States, under the guise of that symbolic garden hose that the United States was lending to the British, would be used to put out more than one fire. The British received more than $1 billion in Lend-Lease aid through October of 1941. Roosevelt expanded the program in April 1941 so that the same process could provide assistance to China in its fight against Japan. The Americans took over the responsibility of providing defense for Iceland, relieving the British military of that task. The U.S. also began protecting the convoys, Canadian and British, between Iceland and Canada. An American destroyer depth-charged a German U-boat during a September 1941 convoy escort.

To Germany, these actions did not seem to be in keeping with their concept of neutrality, and Admiral Dönitz intended to show the Americans what it meant to challenge the U-boat fleet. In October 1941, a U-boat wolf pack torpedoed an American destroyer during an attack on a convoy in the Western North Atlantic. The destroyer survived, but 11 crew members did not. On October 31 of that year, the USS *Reuben James* was sunk by a U-boat, with a loss of 115 members of the crew.

After the Japanese attack on Pearl Harbor, the United States entered the war, no longer neutral, and Lend-Lease continued. As the Americans mobilized, Lend-Lease aircraft, weapons, and vehicles were sent to Allies who were already in the fight. In late 1941 and 1942, Lend-Lease was expanded to aid the Soviet Union, passing supplies through the Arctic Convoys, Persian Corridor, and the Alaska-Siberia Air Route.

Great Britain kept much of the equipment it had used during the war and purchased the items for ten cents on the dollar after the war ended. The total value of the loan came to approximately £1,075 million; this loan, which was paid off in 2006, provided more than $31 billion worth of supplies for the British during World War II.

The other Lend-Lease recipients benefitted both during and after the war as well. Because the nations at war were focusing on producing the weapons that their soldiers needed in order to fight, they reduced the manufacture of other needed items. Thanks to Lend-Lease, the nations received food, munitions, trucks, and transport aircraft. In addition to the 2,000 trains that the Soviets would receive from Lend-Lease so that they could deliver supplies to their soldiers on the front lines, they received trucks which were still in use when the war ended. Although the United States and the Soviet Union would evolve from wary allies to bitter enemies after the war, Lend-Lease provided needed support for the Russians who were bearing the brunt of the war on the Eastern Front.

The Lend-Lease program that was decried by American isolationists was the foundation for the close bond between the United States and Europe that would build through the ensuing years of war against the Germans. When the war ended, that bond among the Western nations would grow into a strong partnership of countries dedicated to maintaining peace and nurturing democracy. Seen in that perspective, Lend-Lease was a bargain.

Chapter Four

The High Point of the U-boats

"It appeared possible that we should not be able to regard convoy as an effective system of defence."

—Royal Navy Report

Admiral Dönitz did not waste any time in sending his U-boats to the Atlantic coast of the United States after the Americans entered the war in December 1941. Events had taken place with such rapidity that the United States was suddenly cast from its neutrality into the heart of the war. In the midst of the confusion that followed its entry into the war, the United States Navy neglected to act upon intelligence obtained by the British that Admiral Dönitz planned to launch Operation Drumbeat to send a significant contingent of his U-boats to the eastern shores of the United States.

It must have seemed like easy pickings for the U-boats. The Americans didn't set blackouts along the eastern coast, nor did the United States form convoys along the shore. By the end of January 1942, 53 U-boats had sent 100 Allied ships to the bottom of the Atlantic, and most of those ships were attacked off the East Coast of America. For the Germans, this was the U-boat's second "happy time" as they exploited the vulnerability of the unescorted American merchant ships.

Realizing the need to provide defense for their merchant ships, the U.S. put a convoy system in place in 1942, and in response, the U-boats withdrew to the mid-Atlantic that summer. Both sides experienced heavy losses in the battles waged between the escorts and the U-boats. Admiral Max Horton became commander-in-chief of the Western Approaches Command in November 1942, and he added to the convoy escorts as more vessels became available. These ships, because they were not specifically tied to convoy defense, were able to hunt U-boats.

The year 1943 began with a continuation of the peril upon the Atlantic. Great Britain faced a dire situation with low supply levels because of the mounting Allied shipping losses; the Germans were sinking ships faster than the Allies could build new ones. Determined to deal a death blow to the supply lifeline keeping the Allies in the war, Dönitz sent all of his U-boats into the Atlantic. The convoys were daunted by the threat of the U-boat attacks. Churchill made the decision to cancel the next planned outgoing and returning convoys. Roosevelt disagreed with Churchill's decision; the convoys, he said, needed to sail whenever possible.

The German Kriegsmarine's wolf pack tactics made the U-boats a deadly force in the Atlantic as they set simultaneous surface attacks at night, a time which was much more effective for them because, during the day, the patrolling Allied aircraft overhead limited their ability to converge on the convoys. The winter season provided extended periods of darkness in the North Atlantic, concealing the submarine operations as they surfaced. The winter of 1942-1943 saw the greatest number of submarines sent to the mid-Atlantic, this at a time when comprehensive anti-submarine aircraft were not yet patrolling that part of the ocean.

March 1943 was the height of the U-boat offensive in the Battle of the Atlantic, with a total loss of 82 long ton ships compared to only 12 U-boats at the same time. According to a report from the British Navy, Germany "never came so near to disrupting communications between the New World and the Old as in the first twenty days of March 1943."

The U-boats in the water were as deadly as the German blitzkrieg on land. SC 122, an eastbound convoy of 60 ships on the route from New York to Liverpool, set sail on March 5, 1943, with one destroyer and five corvettes from the Western Local Escort Force. Bad weather forced two ships to return to New York on March 6; on March 8, six more ships were forced back to Halifax. On March 13, the remaining ships in the convoy changed escorts off Cape Race. Mid-Ocean Escort Force B5 Escort Group replaced the original escorts, bringing eight warships: the destroyers HMS *Havelock* and USS *Upshur*; the River-class frigate HMS *Swale*; the Flower-class corvettes *Lavender*, *Pimpernel*, *Buttercup*, *Godetia*, and *Saxifrage*, and a trawler as rescue vessel.

Also headed east, HX 229 sailed from New York on March 8 with 40 ships. On March 9, 34 more ships sailed as HX 229A; they had originally been part of HX 229 but were delayed in sailing because of heavy traffic in New York. On March 14, HX 229 met its Mid-Ocean Escort

Force, which consisted of four destroyers and a corvette. The commander, G.J. Luther of the HMS *Volunteer*, was only on his second crossing. The B4 Escort Group included destroyers HMS *Beverley, Mansfield,* and *Witherington,* and the corvette *Anemone*. On March 15, the *Witherington* was replaced by the corvette *Pennywort*.

The German signals intelligence group had alerted the U-boats that an Allied convoy was on its way; by March 13, intelligence knew the location of SC 122. Dönitz was eager for the opportunity to attack a convoy on its way east, with a full cargo of materials heading for Europe and the entire width of the Air Gap to cross. Three patrol lines, or rakes, of submarines were waiting: the *Raubgraf* ("Robber Baron") was sent to patrol the western edge of the Air Gap off eastern Newfoundland; *Stürmer* ("Daredevil") had 18 new boats lined up in the middle of the Air Gap; three of the boats had already engaged with SC 121; to the east of *Stürmer* was *Dränger* ("Harrier") and its 11 boats.

Raubgraf was ordered by Admiral Dönitz to intercept and form a new rake to the west. Owing to the wind from the west, SC 122 passed *Raubgraf* 24 hours before the patrol line had formed. A message from one of the U-boats revealed its location, and the convoy SC 122 was able to avoid the area where the U-boats were assembled.

Because the Germans had broken Allied Cipher Number Three, the U-boats could be placed where convoy HX 229 would be easy prey. However, bad weather during the night of March 15 into early March 16 allowed HX 229 to pass through the *Raubgraf* patrol line without being sighted. When morning came, *U-653*, which was returning to base due to mechanical problems, spotted HX 229 heading east. Dönitz sent *Raubgraf* to pursue and intercept; *Stürmer* and *Dränger* were instructed to head west to form a new line ahead of the convoy.

On the evening of March 16, *Raubgraf* caught up with HX 229 and attacked, sinking three ships; the following morning, five more ships sank within a span of only eight hours. Two escort ships dropped out so that they could rescue survivors, leaving the convoy weakened and lacking protection. Although the escorts attempted to chase and attack the U-boats, they met with failure.

U-boat *U-338*, located on the northeastern end of the *Stürmer* patrol line, spotted SC 122 on its way east, 120 miles away from HX 229. The U-boat attacked and quickly sank four ships, damaging a fifth so badly that it sank later that day. HX 229 lost two more ships during the day. Midday on March 17, two of the *Stürmer* U-boats were able to get through the escort defenses but were held off thanks to Very Long Range (VLR) aircraft. SC 122 also fended off attacks.

With the two convoys only 70 miles apart, the U-boat attacks continued at night. *U-338* met with a counter-attack by the escorts but was able to sink SC 122's freighter, *Granville*. After midnight, two more ships, *Port Auckland* and *Zouave* met their demise from *U-305*. The fighting went on; HX 229 lost more ships but was reinforced on March 19. Attacks continued taking place during the night, but the damage was for the most part minimal. Realizing that he had achieved as much as he could hope for, Admiral Dönitz abandoned the attack. The largest convoy battle of the war was over, and Germany had come out victorious, only losing one U-boat while sinking 22 Allied ships.

The March attacks had caused enough damage that many boats had to be withdrawn from action for repairs, but that didn't mean that the action ceased for those still engaged. Churchill saw this as the final proof that the Allied escorts were stretched too thin and placing too great a strain on the Royal Navy. Despite Roosevelt's wish for the convoys to keep going, he was sympathetic to the decision by Churchill to postpone convoys to the Arctic at the end of March, with no plans to sail again until the autumn. At this point, Russia was suffering the lack of supplies; the Eastern Front was a brutal campaign, and Stalin needed tanks in order to keep the tide of battle turning in the Allies' favor.

Known as Black May, May of 1943 would bring a different reckoning to the Battle of the Atlantic. The attack by *U-515* on convoy TS 37 caused the loss of four tankers within three minutes. Over the next six hours, three more tankers would be lost. The turning point came when convoy ONS 5 was heading from Great Britain to North America. The battle over this convoy involved more than 50 Allied ships and escorts against more than 40 U-boats. Both sides suffered heavy losses—thirteen Allied ships and six German U-boats—but the tide for the Allies was about to turn. The next three convoys lost seven ships, the same number that the Germans lost in U-boats. Then, when convoy SC 130 encountered a pack of 25 U-boats, the convoy didn't lose any ships, and the Germans lost three U-boats. Serving on one of the U-boats that sank was Peter Dönitz, son of Admiral Dönitz.

Subsequently, Dönitz ordered his U-boat force to leave the Atlantic to recoup. They lacked the numbers to return to fighting in force until the autumn. When they did return, they would never again dominate the fighting as they had in the earlier years. May of 1943 saw the U-boats reach their peak of dominance and also their doom as 41 were lost, amounting to 25% of the force. As the Allies lost fewer ships and crew members, the U-boats lost more: 18 to convoy battles and 14 to air patrols, leading Admiral Dönitz's decision to order a temporary halt to the German U-boat campaign.

The year 1943 witnessed a change in the tide of the battles on land and at sea, as the Allies began to sense that they might be able to defeat the Germans. What caused the change in fortune? In part, it was a case of practice makes perfect: the escorts and escort groups were gaining in expertise. Technology and weaponry were improving. A new tactic known as the "creeping attack," which stationed support groups at sea so that they could pursue U-boats when convoys were being attacked, gave the convoys the flexibility to be aggressive. But most important was the breakthrough in deciphering the "unbreakable code," the German naval Enigma machine.

Chapter Five

The Codebreakers of the Battle of the Atlantic

"At that juncture, Turing made his fantastic achievement of breaking naval Enigma. There was no other salvation for Britain. Once naval Enigma was broken, the sinkings dropped by 75 percent."

—Captain Jerry Roberts

After the fall of France in 1940, Great Britain was the only player left standing, and the British were being driven to their knees. The U-boats had turned the Atlantic Ocean into a hazard zone; the wolf packs knew where the convoys would be, but the British had no idea where the wolf packs were lurking. The British were in danger of losing the war. What would assist them in winning it, at this point in the conflict, was not tanks or ships or planes. The brains of Bletchley Park made the difference between victory and defeat.

Movies, books, and television programs have celebrated the wizardry of the Bletchley Park codebreakers who were able to break Enigma, the German code that the Nazis regarded as unbreakable. The Germans had already broken the British Navy's codes, and this was a huge benefit to their effectiveness in the Battle of the Atlantic. The

Germans got an early start on intelligence; they had been preparing for war against Great Britain since the 1930s and were well aware that in order for the Third Reich to dominate Europe, it was necessary to take naval supremacy away from the British Empire.

While the navies were conducting their martial actions, an intellectual battle was taking place on land in England. Decrypting the Morse codes of the enemy was a fierce contest. That a byproduct of the engagement would lead to the development of the first programmable electronic computer demonstrates the far-reaching stakes of the struggle. But in the beginning, it was a battle of wits.

The signals intelligence or SIGINT battle sought to break the ciphers used by the German radioteletype equipment. Radio-derived signals intelligence depended upon the use of radio for centralized command; this was true for both sides. Code-breaking relied upon specialized machines that were capable of mechanical sorting. Ultra, the code name for the British SIGINT operation, utilized complicated and covert activities to intercept and decrypt the high-frequency radio Morse code and teletype traffic. British radio intercept sites extended across the nation to manually record the coded radio signals from the Germans; these messages were sent to a hidden center and decoded by intelligence centers.

For its own part, the German Kriegsmarine understood the importance of code-breaking and the vital intelligence it could produce. As early as the mid-1930s, the German Navy's signals intelligence unit had broken some of the Royal Navy's most important codes. B-Dienst or the Beobachter Dienst was Germany's naval radio SIGINT service. B-Dienst had a network of intercept sites that forwarded the coded messages from the British and sent them to its headquarters in Berlin. There, the messages were decrypted, and their revelations were used to further Germany's military strategy.

The Kriegsmarine's communication staff was ambitious to develop an encrypted radio communications system capable of controlling a substantial fleet at war. They found their answer in the commercial encryption device known as Enigma, which had been marketed in 1923 so that businesses could protect themselves from industrial espionage. Noticing that Germany was investing in Enigma, Poland, wary of their neighbors' interest in defying the Versailles Treaty and building up their military for expansion, began paying closer attention to what was going on.

The Enigma machine looked like a big typewriter with an alphabetical keyboard. On the top of the machine was another alphabet. As one letter was typed on the keyboard, a different letter lit up on the alphabet on the top of the machine. The pressure imposed on the keyboard letter created an electrical connection that made the second letter light up, due to complex wiring with an almost unlimited number of potential outcomes. Cipher clerks were also able to decode these messages using the Enigma machine. Once the machine had been set up, the clerk would type the characters of the message that had been received; meanwhile, a colleague would record the letter that lit up at each keystroke. When the typing was done, the message would be written in understandable German.

The task that faced the Poles in attempting to decrypt German military radio message traffic was formidable. In order to decrypt the messages, the Poles had to reconstruct the typing and encryption process that was taking place inside the Enigma. One estimate asserts that there were a thousand trillion potential outcomes for the codes. Using the commercial version of the Enigma machine as a starting point, the Polish mathematicians began an effort to break the German encryption system—an effort that benefited from cooperation with their French counterparts, as the French provided several documents they had obtained covertly from a spy.

During 1938, the year before the Nazi invasion of Poland, the Poles were able to reconstruct the Enigma keys thanks to the clues they had received from the French. But in September 1938, the Germans added two new unique wheels for each Enigma which made the task of discerning the keys more complicated. The Poles were not deterred; they were developing their own machine to break the daily key settings of the Germans. Their invention, a forerunner of the punch-card sorting machines that would become well known in the early decades after the war ended, had the ability to calculate all the potential keys that would otherwise have had to be checked manually. Known as the *bomba*, the machine developed by the Poles—while it did use some of the very same processes that Enigma used—could not handle the more complicated alternatives of the later-version Enigma.

In July 1939, the Polish codebreakers met with the British so that they could hasten the Allies' work to break the Enigma's code. Today, the name of Alan Turing is well known as the father of modern computer science. But in the early days of World War II, he was just a shy mathematician at Bletchley Park; brilliant, certainly, and quirky (owing to his allergies, he wore a gas mask while riding his bicycle). The Polish mathematicians who had been working on the decoded Enigma messages had shared their findings with the British, but once war broke out, the Germans changed their cipher system on a daily basis, complicating the effort to understand the coded messages. Turing's work on his bombe (based on the Poles' bomba machine) enabled the British to read the messages sent from the German Navy, eventually making it possible for the Allied convoys to elude the U-boats. Sadly, Turing's later life led to scandal in the England of the 1950s where homosexuality was a crime. He lost his security clearances and was convicted at trial in 1952. Alan Turing died two years later; the cause of death was ruled suicide.

During his lifetime, Turing's tremendous contribution to the war and his legacy in furthering the advance of computer science did not achieve the renown that might be expected of such an intellectual giant. The complete story of the activities that went on at Bletchley Park and the codebreakers who worked tirelessly to crack the German code was not fully known until the 1990s. It's been estimated that the accomplishments of the codebreakers shortened the duration of the war by several years, saving an untold number of lives in the process.

The Battle of the Atlantic was a phenomenal victory for the British military. It was no less a crowning achievement for the civilian codebreakers. Democracy, a fragile treasure in the decades after World War I, was in mortal jeopardy during World War II. As Germany promoted its military might and its theories of the Aryan race as superior to other ethnic groups, the Nazis built concentration camps to imprison and murder people who failed to conform to its own narrow views of what constituted a super race. The camps not only included Jews who were rounded up and send to their deaths merely because of their ethnic background; the Nazis also condemned the physically and mentally disabled, members of Slavic ethnicity, the Gypsies or Roma, and homosexuals.

It is ironic that Alan Turing, whose sexual orientation would have sent him to a Nazi concentration camp, was the man responsible for cracking the unbreakable code, the Enigma, which enabled the Allies to win the Battle of the Atlantic.

Conclusion

The Battle of the Atlantic, the longest campaign of World War II, took place upon the Atlantic Ocean as the Allies traveled back and forth from North America to Great Britain with desperately needed oil, provisions, weapons, and supplies for the embattled forces fighting against Nazi Germany. The U-boats, the terror of the undersea, made those convoy journeys particularly hazardous, especially after Germany's Admiral Karl Dönitz developed the wolf pack strategy, in which a group of U-boats suddenly surfaced together to bring down convoy ships.

From the start of the war on September 3, 1939 until May 8, 1945, the Battle of the Atlantic was fought to keep the Germans from blockading the Atlantic Ocean. The efforts of those valiant seafarers would make D-Day possible, but there were times when even Winston Churchill feared that the prowess of the U-boats would imperil the Allies in their battle against the Nazi menace that had conquered Western Europe. The bravery of the Allied naval crews, and the brilliance of the Bletchley Park codebreakers, prevented the Atlantic Ocean from becoming yet another victim of Nazi dominance.

The significance of the Battle of the Atlantic cannot be understated. As Winston Churchill noted after World War II had ended, "The Battle of the Atlantic was the dominating factor all through the war. Never for one moment could we forget that everything happening elsewhere, on land at sea or in the air, depended ultimately on its outcome."

Printed in Great Britain
by Amazon